Who Are The Rolling Stones?

by Dana Meachen Rau

illustrated by Andrew Thomson

Penguin Workshop

To Derek—DMR

To Rhia—AT

PENGUIN WORKSHOP
An imprint of Penguin Random House LLC, New York

Published by Penguin Workshop, an imprint of Penguin Random House LLC, New York.
PENGUIN and PENGUIN WORKSHOP are trademarks of Penguin Books Ltd.
WHO HQ & Design is a registered trademark of Penguin Random House LLC.
Printed in the USA.

Visit us online at www.penguinrandomhouse.com.

Library of Congress Control Number: 2017941419

ISBN 9781101995587 10 9 8 7 6 5 4 3 WRZL

Contents

Who Are the Rolling Stones?

In October of 1961, eighteen-year-old Mick Jagger was on his way to class at the London School of Economics. Music was often on his mind. This day was no different. He had a few records under his arm to show his friends at college.

Even though Mick lived in England, he listened to American music. He liked the blues—an old type of music that often had a slow beat and sad lyrics. He also liked rock and roll, a very new type with a faster beat and lots of energy.

On the Dartford station platform, Mick noticed another teenager. It was his old friend Keith Richards from grade school. Mick noticed that Keith was carrying a guitar case. Keith saw the records that Mick was holding. They started talking. Keith loved American music, too!

Mick was a singer. Keith was a guitar player. Following their meeting that day—and their early friendships with Brian Jones, Bill Wyman, and Charlie Watts—a powerful rock-and-roll band was born.

The Rolling Stones blended blues and rock and roll into a unique sound. They soon became famous in their home country of England. Teenagers in America became fans, too.

Eventually, the Rolling Stones became the greatest rock-and-roll band in the world. They have been together for more than fifty years—longer than any other band in history. Since Mick and Keith met on the train platform in 1961, a lot has changed. But through it all, the band has always worked hard to do what they love best—play music.

And all their hard work has paid off. When people think of rock and roll, they think of the Rolling Stones.

CHAPTER 1
Starting Out

Keith Richards and Mick Jagger were both born in 1943 in the town of Dartford, England.

The country was in the middle of fighting World War II at the time. And Dartford had been the site of many bombings during the war. The fighting ended in 1945. But throughout their childhoods, Keith and Mick's neighborhood was still piled with crumbled pieces of bombed buildings.

Keith and Mick lived in the same neighborhood and went to elementary school together. But they were not close friends. Mick was outgoing, and Keith was quiet. Mick was a good student. Keith hated school. When their families moved to opposite ends of Dartford, the boys didn't keep in touch.

As they grew older, they each developed a love of music. When Mick was fourteen, he got his first guitar. He spent a lot of time listening to music on the radio. In the mid-1950s, most people still listened to the same type of music their parents had before the war. But Mick tuned the dial to faraway stations in Luxembourg and Germany that broadcast American music.

Then Mick got a record player. Shops in England didn't always carry the music he wanted. So he ordered music directly from the United States. His records came mainly from Chess Records in Chicago, Illinois. Chess was a recording studio that worked with Muddy Waters, Chuck Berry, and other American musicians that Mick liked.

On the other side of Dartford, Keith was greatly influenced by his musical family—especially by his grandfather, who had been a bandleader and had played guitar. Keith got his first guitar as a present for his fifteenth birthday. He, too, listened to American musicians and singers, like Chuck Berry and Elvis Presley, on the radio.

He sometimes hid his small radio in his bedcovers so he could listen to music at night. Even though his radio didn't always get good reception, he heard something new and exciting in American music. It was the beginnings of rock and roll. "The music came across the airwaves, and suddenly it felt as if the world was actually changing," Keith said.

In 1961, Mick was in college. Keith was a student at an art school. They each rode the train to get to their classes. One day in the fall, they ran into each other at the Dartford train station. They started talking about music. They realized they had a lot in common.

Mick and Keith's American Music

Blues is a style of music that developed in the American South in the early 1900s. Its songs are made up of a certain pattern of repeated lines and rhythms. The term "blues" refers to the sadness of the lyrics and the sound of the music. Some of the most famous American blues musicians are Robert Johnson, Howlin' Wolf, Muddy Waters, and B.B. King.

In the 1940s, blues moved from the South to northern American cities. It developed into rhythm and blues, a style with more of a dance beat, more instruments, and often happier lyrics.

Then in the 1950s, musicians mixed rhythm and blues and other music styles to create rock and roll. Rock and roll had lots of energy. Most adults didn't like it, but it was popular with teenagers. Chuck Berry, Little Richard, and Elvis Presley were some of the early pioneers of rock and roll.

So the boys started spending more time together. They shared records and played their guitars. Mick was already in a band called Little Boy Blue and the Blue Boys, along with a friend named Dick Taylor. Keith knew Dick from art school. And soon Keith joined the band, too. They played at school dances and other small events.

The three friends visited blues clubs any chance they had. In the spring of 1962, they went to the Ealing Club outside of London. Onstage that night, they heard a teenager named Brian Jones playing guitar.

Brian had grown up in Cheltenham—a wealthier community than Mick and Keith's hometown of Dartford. He was a year older than they were. Brian had done well in school and sports, and he showed an early talent for music. But he was also a troublemaker. He sometimes skipped school to practice his saxophone and clarinet He was a blues fan, too. And soon, they all had become friends.

Brian Jones

Brian, Mick, Keith, and Dick decided to form their own band. They advertised for more musicians. They held auditions. And the new group came together: Mick sang, Keith and Brian played guitar, Dick played bass, and Ian Stewart played piano. They used different drummers for different shows. They called themselves the Rollin' Stones. They took the name from a song recorded in 1950 by the famous blues musician Muddy Waters.

The Rollin' Stones played together for the first time on July 12, 1962, at London's Marquee Club. The Marquee Club was in the basement of a movie theater. It was an old dance hall that had been turned into a jazz club. The band played rhythm-and-blues and rock-and-roll cover songs.

Muddy Waters (1913–1983)

Muddy Waters's real name was McKinley Morganfield. He got the nickname Muddy Waters because he had grown up in a small town along the Mississippi River.

As a young child, Muddy played the harmonica. When he was a teenager, he switched to guitar.

He liked to play southern blues music, sometimes called the Delta blues because it developed near the Mississippi River Delta. In 1943, he moved to Chicago. He mixed the blues sound he loved from home with the more modern electric guitar. He was a leader in this new type of music that people called the Chicago blues.

In 1958, Muddy Waters traveled to England. Soon, people all over the world were hearing and loving his unique sound. His use of electric guitar to play the blues is often considered to be the link between the blues and rock and roll. Muddy Waters is a legendary influence on the history of modern music.

Cover songs are tunes that have been written and already recorded by other artists. The younger members of the audience seemed to really enjoy the music. But a few of the older jazz fans thought their sound was just terrible.

The Rollin' Stones' hope of playing together as a band in front of an audience had come true. They were all talented musicians. But were they good enough to last?

CHAPTER 2
The Band's Big Break

The Rollin' Stones spent most of their time together. In August 1962, Mick and Keith decided to move out of their childhood homes in Dartford. They joined Brian in a London apartment. They couldn't afford much. The apartment had only two rooms and was lit with bare lightbulbs. The boys owned no furniture except for a few mattresses to sleep on. They left their trash on the floor and dishes piled in the sink. It was especially freezing in winter.

Mick was still in college at the London School of Economics. He and Keith were only nineteen years old, and Brian was twenty. Brian and Keith now devoted all of their time to the band. Brian worked hard to find them places to play. But jobs were hard to get. Not enough people wanted to hear a bunch of British teenagers singing their own versions of American songs.

Dick Taylor decided to leave the band. So the Rollin' Stones began looking for a new bass player. Bill Wyman was about seven years older than the other boys and already had a steady job and a family of his own. When Bill showed up at the audition,

Bill Wyman

the Stones could tell right away that he was talented. Bill had experience playing with rock-and-roll bands. He also had his own amplifier—a great addition to the band!

The Stones also had their eye on Charlie Watts. They had seen him perform many times at the Ealing Club and hoped he would become their full-time drummer. Charlie had grown up playing his drum set along with jazz records. He was a jazz expert. At first, he wasn't sure about joining the Rollin' Stones.

Charlie Watts

He kept his day job at an advertising agency, just in case drumming for the band didn't work out. But by January 1963, Charlie was in.

Once in a while, the Rollin' Stones would be invited to play at the Marquee Club in London. Larger crowds and eager fans started to fill the dance floor. But the band still hoped for their "big break"—a lucky chance that would make them popular enough to launch their music career.

A man named Giorgio Gomelsky had just opened a new club. But the "club" was only the dark back room of a hotel in Richmond, a town outside of London. One Sunday night, the club's regular band couldn't make it. Giorgio knew that Brian Jones had started a band and needed work. So he asked the Stones to fill in.

The Rollin' Stones first played at the club—called the Crawdaddy—on February 24, 1963. It was a snowy day. Only a few people came out for the show. By the next week, the crowd doubled. Even more people showed up the week after that. Pretty soon, people had to line up outside in the early afternoon for a show that didn't start until seven o'clock. Giorgio was happy with the packed house. He booked the Stones to play there every week for eight months. The Rollin' Stones finally had a regular job! They played a lot of their favorite tunes by popular American musicians like Jimmy Reed, Muddy Waters, and Bo Diddley.

The band was especially good at connecting with their audience. As they sang and played, their fans went wild. The crowd waved their hands, jumped around, and danced on tables. This was sometimes a problem in the tiny club—it was so crowded, the dancing was more like sweating, shaking, and wiggling in place.

Mick liked to dance when he sang. But there wasn't much room on the stage at the Crawdaddy. So instead of dancing, he shook his head to the music. Even those small moves got the crowd excited. Keith later said, "Mick could make an awful lot out of a couple of square feet."

The members of the band worked well together. Brian was the clear leader. He made all of the decisions for the band. Mick was the lead singer, connecting most with the audience. Keith liked to experiment with new music. Bill and Charlie were good musicians and dependable, and always supported the rest of their bandmates. Ian was a solid piano player and friend.

During their shows at the Crawdaddy, the Stones learned a lot about playing and performing in front of an audience. They made mistakes. But they realized that good shows and bad shows were both chances to get better. Mick once said, "We played everything and anything—that's how you learn."

The Rollin' Stones were finally getting noticed. Their regular job at the Crawdaddy gave them the time to become better musicians. It also gave them a chance to build up a group of young fans. The more fans they had, the bigger their audiences would be, and their popularity could only grow from there.

CHAPTER 3
Creating an Image

By 1963, the Beatles had become the most popular band in England. One night in April, the four members of the Beatles came to see the Rollin' Stones play at the Crawdaddy. They hung out with the Stones afterward and talked about music. When the Stones went to see the Beatles perform live, Brian was especially impressed by the way girls screamed in excitement whenever the Beatles appeared. He wanted the Stones to be superstars like the Beatles.

The Beatles

The four members of the Beatles—John Lennon, Paul McCartney, George Harrison, and Ringo Starr—were originally from Liverpool, England. They loved American rock and roll. They formed their own band in the early 1960s and quickly became popular in England and Germany. By 1964, they were famous all over the world.

Their huge popularity was known as "Beatlemania." The Beatles were young, funny, and handsome. Teenagers loved them. Girls often screamed so loudly at concerts that the members of the band couldn't even hear themselves play.

The band broke up after spending less than ten years together. But John, Paul, George, and Ringo all went on to have successful solo careers. The Beatles are the best-selling band in music history and one of the most important rock bands of all time.

Not long after the Beatles came to the Crawdaddy, a tall, stylish young man showed up to hear the Stones play. Andrew Oldham was only nineteen years old, younger than any members of the Stones. But he already had a lot of connections in the music world. He had even worked for the Beatles! He liked the Rollin' Stones' sound and wanted to be

Andrew Oldham

their manager. The band signed a contract with Andrew. Soon after that, their new manager got the Stones a record deal with Decca Records.

The Rollin' Stones were becoming known as a talented London band. But Andrew Oldham had bigger dreams for them. He wanted to make some changes. Andrew didn't think Ian Stewart had the right look. He wasn't as young as the rest of the band. So Andrew fired him. Ian still acted as the band's road manager and played piano for concerts and albums for many years to come. But he was no longer an official member of the Rollin' Stones. Next, Andrew added a *g* to the end of the band's name, so they were now called the Rolling Stones. He asked them to wear matching outfits for photo shoots, just like the Beatles did.

The Rolling Stones recorded their first single—a cover of their idol Chuck Berry's song

“Come On.” It was released on June 7, 1963, and rose to number twenty-one on the British music charts.

Soon, the band appeared on British television shows. They were interviewed for newspaper articles.

They gave up trying to be like the Beatles with their trimmed hair, similar clothes, and friendly smiles. Instead, the Stones wanted to be themselves. They dressed how they wanted. They let their hair grow long and shaggy. They didn't always smile in photographs. They said whatever they wanted in interviews, and they weren't concerned about being polite.

Teenagers loved their rude attitude. Adults called them cavemen. The more attention they received—both good and bad—the more popular they became.

That August, Mick and Keith moved in with Andrew Oldham. Brian started to feel jealous. He worried that the others were trying to take over *his* band. But all the band members were willing to work hard to make the Rolling Stones a success. Charlie and Bill finally left their regular jobs to devote all of their time to the band. Mick left school. Their lives were headed in a new direction. The band was really taking off.

The Rolling Stones were popular enough to play shows every night of the week. They traveled all over England, sleeping in their van when they were on the road. Their songs rose up the British charts and even broke into the top 50 in the United States.

CLUB88
STAGE
ONLY.!

By April 1964, they had released their first album, a collection of cover songs, called simply *The Rolling Stones.* It sold one hundred thousand copies the first week it was on sale and took the number-one spot away from the Beatles! The Rolling Stones were now the *new* hottest band in England.

CHAPTER 4
Growing Success

The Rolling Stones were a huge hit in Britain. In May 1964, their album was released in the United States under the name *England's Newest Hitmakers*. The very next month they would begin their first US tour.

The Stones were excited to come to America. But not all Americans were excited to see them.

American audiences expected the Stones to be like the Beatles, who had recently toured the United States. When the Beatles played their American shows, they stood still and smiled onstage, played their instruments, and sang songs like "I Want to Hold Your Hand." But the Stones were very different from the Beatles. They didn't dress alike for their performances.

Mick wiggled and danced around the stage. Adults thought the band seemed tough and scary. Some people even made fun of them. One journalist wrote, "The Beatles want to hold your hand, but the Stones want to burn down your town."

The British Invasion

The Beatles came to America to perform for the first time in February 1964. Their instant fame opened the way for other British bands to find success in the United States throughout the 1960s.

The Rolling Stones arrived in the United States in June. Then the Who, the Kinks, the Animals, Herman's Hermits, and many other bands followed. The songs of the British bands knocked American songs off the music charts. This rock-and-roll takeover became known as the British Invasion.

For most of their fifteen-day tour, the band played to very small audiences. They were hoping to "make it big" in America. But the United States was much larger than England. It had more radio stations and more people to buy records. Becoming famous in America would take more time. The tour was certainly helping. They just had to be patient.

Back home in England, the Stones didn't have to worry about playing to small crowds. Their concerts were filled with screaming fans. Some of their shows had even become dangerous. When they arrived at theaters and clubs, fans mobbed their car and pounded on the windows. The band needed police to help them get from their car into the building. Even while they played, fans rushed onto the stage.

The Rolling Stones returned to America for another tour in October. By this time, only four short months later, even more people had heard of the Stones. Besides playing in concerts, they also appeared on *The Ed Sullivan Show*. Millions of Americans tuned in to watch. But the next day,

angry parents called and sent telegrams to the television station. They called the performance trash. They thought the band looked like slobs. Ed Sullivan apologized and said that he would never have the Stones back on his show again.

While in the States, the Stones had plans to appear in a concert called T.A.M.I. (Teen Age Music International) in California. They were going to perform with some very famous musicians, including Chuck Berry, Marvin Gaye, the Beach Boys, and Smokey Robinson. Everyone in the band was nervous to go onstage after the talented soul singer and dancer James Brown.

James Brown

His live performances were legendary for their energy and showmanship. But after the Stones played the last act of the show, Mr. Brown himself complimented them on a job well done.

In early 1965, the Rolling Stones also toured Australia, New Zealand, and the Netherlands. Now that the band was doing so well, their manager, Andrew Oldham, wanted Mick and Keith to begin writing their own songs.

Mick and Keith soon discovered that they made a great songwriting team. They seemed to be the most creative while they were touring.

Moves Like Jagger

Throughout his career, Mick Jagger has been known for his fancy footwork, bendable body, and nonstop energy. In the beginning, when he had played with the Blue Boys, he used to roll around on the floor. During early club shows with the Rolling Stones, he wiggled, dipped, and spun. He practiced in front of mirrors. After he saw James Brown perform his twirls, drops, and splits at a live show, Mick practiced *his* moves, too.

They often wrote on the tour bus and in hotel rooms. Keith would work out a tune on the guitar. Mick would try out different lyrics to fit the tune.

On their third American tour, in the spring of 1965, they wrote what would become the Rolling Stones' most famous song. One morning, Keith woke up to find that the cassette player next to his bed was at the end of the tape. He rewound it and listened. Keith had recorded himself in the middle of the night playing a short bit of music on his guitar. The tune was then followed by the sound of snoring as he fell back asleep.

At their Florida hotel, Keith played the tune for Mick. Keith said, "The words that go with this are, 'I can't get no—satisfaction.'" They worked together on the rest of the tune and lyrics. While still on tour, the Stones went into the studio to record their new song. They worked through the night until it was finished.

"(I Can't Get No) Satisfaction" became the band's first megahit—number one in the United States, and then number one in the entire world. The Rolling Stones had conquered America. And they were on top of music charts around the globe.

CHAPTER 5
Rough Roads

After "Satisfaction" dominated the music charts in the summer of 1965, the Rolling Stones became a huge success. Their schedule was packed with tours, television appearances, and recording sessions. Ed Sullivan even broke his promise and invited the Stones back to perform on his show. They had no time to rest.

By July of that year, the Rolling Stones had sold about ten million singles and about five million albums. They were rich! They spent money on fancy cars, fancy clothes, and fancy houses. They had become rock stars.

The Stones loved driving their fans wild, just like they had back at the Crawdaddy Club. But sometimes the audiences weren't just dancing to the music. They were out of control. Inside the theaters, fans threw things at the band, ripped up seats, and tried to grab them onstage.

Outside, fans became violent, overturning cars and smashing windows. After many Stones shows, people often had to be rushed to the hospital. Their concerts were becoming unsafe.

The band members lived a dangerous life when they weren't performing, too. They held wild parties. They destroyed hotel rooms. Most of them drank alcohol and took drugs.

In the fall of 1966, the Stones wanted a break from their year of nonstop work. They wanted to focus on writing new music. Keith had bought a lot of records during their trips to the United States, and he finally took time to listen to them. The band came into the recording studio with the beginnings of ideas. Then they experimented with rhythm, lyrics,

and instruments. They worked without a plan.

Andrew Oldham, who had been the Stones' manager since the days of the Crawdaddy Club, didn't like the band's new direction. He didn't think they were focused enough. So he decided to stop managing the band.

And then drugs became a big problem for Keith and Mick. In February 1967, police searched Keith's house and found illegal drugs there. Both Keith and Mick were arrested. Newspapers reported the news. Keith and Mick even spent a short time in jail.

Their arrests didn't change the opinions of their fans, though. They still loved the Rolling Stones because the band sang about subjects that teenagers could relate to. They sang about being angry and frustrated. They sang about how hard it was to make choices. The Stones' songs dealt with problems that adults didn't like to discuss.

The 1960s and a Nation Ready for Change

The 1950s was a prosperous time for many Americans. People had jobs and were earning enough money to buy houses, cars, and television sets. But many people, including minorities, poor people, and women, hadn't shared in the successes of the 1950s.

During the 1960s, things began to change. President John F. Kennedy promised to help black Americans. Civil rights leader Martin Luther King Jr. spoke out against laws that kept whites and blacks separate. President Lyndon Johnson created programs to help the poor. Women demanded to be treated fairly and equally to men.

Many older people wanted things to stay the same. They had only good memories of the way things used to be. The younger generation wanted change. And they were ready to make it happen.

Brian Jones had his own problems. He seemed very unhappy, even with all of the band's success. He liked being a rock star, but he was jealous of Mick and Keith. He couldn't write music the way they did. He didn't feel like the leader of the band anymore. He got sick a lot. He wouldn't show up for shows or recording sessions.

He would purposely play a different song when the band played "Satisfaction" in concert. Brian spent time in medical clinics and in court on drug charges.

Even though this was a rough time for the Stones, they were writing some of the biggest hits of their career. One day in 1968, Keith and Mick were playing together. Mick heard the stomping of boots outside in the rain. When Keith explained that it was his gardener "Jumpin' Jack," Mick added the word "Flash!" and a new song was born. "Jumpin' Jack Flash" was released in May. *Rolling Stone* magazine—which was also named after the Muddy Waters song—called it "supernatural Delta blues by way of Swinging London." The song went on to become one of the most recognizable Rolling Stones songs of all time.

People began calling the Rolling Stones the

“world’s greatest rock-and-roll band.” But life wasn’t always easy at the top.

CHAPTER 6
From Bad to Worse

The other band members grew tired of the way Brian was behaving. Even when he did show up for shows or recording sessions, he was often too sick to play. In June 1969, Keith, Mick, and Charlie went to Brian's house and broke the news—they were kicking him out of the band. Brian didn't seem surprised.

With Brian gone, the Rolling Stones needed a new guitar player. They called Mick Taylor.

Mick Taylor

Taylor was a talented guitar player, and they were all impressed with him. He had also grown up loving blues music.

Only a month after being fired from the band, Brian died in his backyard pool. It was not clear if he had been drinking or taking drugs, or if he had drowned by accident. It was a tragedy for the Stones. They had lost a friend. And their fans had lost an amazing musician.

But the Stones had no plans to slow down. They were giving a free concert on July 5, 1969, only two days after Brian's death, at Hyde Park in London. The stage was one of the largest ever built for an outdoor concert in England.

Hundreds of thousands of people came. Before the Stones started playing, they remembered Brian by reading a poem. Then they released thousands of butterflies into the sunny summer sky.

The Stones had big plans for the rest of that year. They recorded their next album, *Let It Bleed*, and left for another US tour. Mick said that the huge hit from this album, "Gimme

Shelter," was "a kind of end-of-the-world song, really." And for many Americans, it felt a bit like the end of the world. The United States was fighting in the Vietnam War, where many soldiers died every day. Americans were gathering to protest the government and its choices.

President John F. Kennedy, Senator Robert F. Kennedy, and civil rights leader Martin Luther King Jr. had all been assassinated. People were angry. The Stones' music reflected the same angry energy.

At the end of the Stones' US tour, the angry feelings expressed in their music became all too real. The final concert of their tour was set up at the Altamont Speedway in California on December 6, 1969. The Rolling Stones arrived by helicopter with a view of the 350,000 fans below. Such a large audience would be hard to handle.

A motorcycle gang was in charge of security—keeping the band and the audience safe. But the mood of the crowd felt dangerous. And the poor choice of security didn't help. The motorcycle gang wasn't keeping the concert peaceful. In fact, they were causing even more trouble by pushing and fighting fans back from the stage.

The Stones started playing. But they had to stop to tell everyone—both the crowd and their own security—to "cool out." As soon as the Stones were done, they rushed to the helicopter and left.

Before the night was over, members of the motorcycle gang had killed a man. In all, four people died at Altamont. Other fans had to be treated for beatings and for drug use. A magazine article called Altamont "perhaps rock and roll's all-time worst day."

CHAPTER 7
Sticking Their Tongues Out

Even though the Altamont concert had been a disaster, it proved that the Rolling Stones could draw huge, record-breaking crowds. By the early 1970s, the Stones had hundreds of thousands of fans. They also earned a lot of money! But they owed taxes to the British government. To avoid even bigger problems, they had to leave England.

Before the band left the country, they finished work on their next album, called *Sticky Fingers.* It was released on their own record label, Rolling Stones Records. The record showed off their new logo—a mouth with its tongue sticking out. The album became number one in both America and Europe. And the Stones gave a farewell tour before they left England for the south of France in April 1971.

A large house that Keith had rented in the south of France became the band's home base. The beautiful old home had a view of the Mediterranean Sea and a private beach. The Stones didn't have to worry about tours. They didn't have to work around other people's schedules. They could take their time and do whatever they wanted.

The Band's Logo

The Rolling Stones logo is a bright red pair of lips, white teeth, and a long tongue. John Pasche created it for the *Sticky Fingers* album. Although Mick wanted an image of the Hindu goddess Kali—the goddess of time, death, and power, often shown with her tongue sticking out—Pasche has said that he got the idea for the Stones' logo the very first time he met Mick Jagger. The designer was inspired by Mick's own, very large, mouth.

So the group relaxed and wrote lots of new music. When they couldn't find a good recording studio nearby, they built one in the basement of Keith's house.

They also used their "Mighty Mobile"—a vehicle that carried all of the portable recording equipment they needed. Soon, the band had enough songs for a double album. *Exile on Main Street* came out in May 1972.

To promote the new album, the Stones set out on their seventh North American tour in a private plane with their logo painted on the side. Then they toured in Europe and Australia. And they even took the time to stop in Jamaica to work on a new album.

Ron Wood

One day in 1974, Mick Taylor told Mick Jagger that he wanted to leave the band and try out some new music. The Stones hoped to hire their friend Ron Wood to replace him. Ron played guitar with the rock band Faces. He was a good musician and a very positive person. He was also a fan of the Stones. Ron Wood left Faces and joined the Stones in 1975.

The Rolling Stones' next tour was announced on May 1, 1975, in New York City. The band set up their equipment on the back of a flatbed truck and played their music on Fifth Avenue.

ROLLING STONES
Tour America

It was a surprising way to get people excited about their new "Tour of the Americas '75."

While on tour, they played in large sports arenas. Charlie Watts helped design the tour's really big stage that opened like a flower with petals that stretched out into the audience.

Speakers and hundreds of lights hung above it. Mick used a wireless microphone, so he could dance around every part of the stage. They used big props and movie screens. The band put on quite a show!

Arena Rock

In the mid-1970s, as rock music became more popular, bands needed to find larger places to play. Sound equipment was better than ever, too, so bands could perform in large sports arenas. Because the spaces were so large, rock bands needed to be sure the fans could see them.

They expanded their concerts to include large screens, costumes, huge props, light shows, and even fireworks. Along with the Rolling Stones, bands such as KISS and Queen were also known for their amazing arena performances.

After a busy few years, Keith was arrested for carrying and using illegal drugs again. And this time, it looked like he might be sent to jail for a long time. Everyone worried about Keith. And they wondered what would happen to the band.

In October 1978, the judge in Keith's trial explained that a Stones fan had told him how kind Keith had been to her at concerts. The fan—who Keith later called "my blind angel"—had helped keep

him out of jail. After performing a free concert for the Canadian National Institute for the Blind, Keith realized that his drug habit was bad for him, for the people who cared for him, and for the band. He vowed to quit using dangerous drugs.

Heading into the 1980s, the band's tours continued to grow. The Stones had been playing together for twenty years. Their original fans still loved them, of course. But because the band added newer types of music—such as disco, funk, and punk—to their rock-and-roll style, their audiences grew to include new and younger fans.

In 1981, their newest album, *Tattoo You*, shot

to number one in both the United States and Great Britain. The tour for *Tattoo You* was the largest they had ever done. They played for more than two hours to full stadiums at each stop. The stage was sixty-five feet wide with extensions that stretched out another eighty feet. Mick had lots of space to show off his dance moves.

About two million fans saw the tour in America. It earned nearly $50 million, plus another $10 million for T-shirts and other merchandise. After that, the band toured Europe and sang to more than a million and a half people there, too.

After the *Tattoo You* tours, the Stones didn't tour together for seven years. But it wasn't because they needed a break from touring. They needed a break from each other.

CHAPTER 8
Trouble with the Glimmer Twins

Mick and Keith had known each other since they were young boys. They were very close. They had played, sang, written songs, and become huge successes together. They produced albums under the name "The Glimmer Twins." But sometimes, even close friendships can have problems.

By the early 1980s, the Rolling Stones weren't getting along. Keith was upset that Mick wasn't working on the next Stones album. Instead, Mick was focused on releasing his own solo albums. Keith decided to work on his own album, too. Instead of speaking to each other, they argued through interviews they gave to newspapers and magazines. Charlie, Bill, and Ron went off to work on their own projects. The band didn't break up. But they didn't work together for a few years.

Ron tried to get Mick and Keith together again. At a London hotel in the spring of 1988, the band finally held a meeting. They agreed to make a new album. The Rolling Stones had become so huge that they couldn't let it end.

Keith said to Mick, "This thing [the band] is bigger than both of us."

At the beginning of 1989, the band met in Barbados, an island nation in the eastern Caribbean. They started making what would be called their "comeback" album. They planned to tour that fall, so there was a lot of work to do. Once they sat down to write songs together again, things clicked into place.

Keith and Mick took a brief break to fly to New York City for an important ceremony. The Rolling Stones became members of the Rock and Roll Hall of Fame. In his thank-you speech, with Mick Taylor, Ron, and Keith by his side, Mick joked that they were receiving the award for twenty-five years of bad behavior!

Rock and Roll Hall of Fame

The Rock and Roll Hall of Fame Foundation welcomed its first members in 1986. They included Chuck Berry, James Brown, and Little Richard—the same musicians that meant so much to the Rolling Stones at the beginning of their own careers.

The Foundation built the Rock and Roll Hall of Fame and Museum in Cleveland, Ohio, in 1995. Its goal is to teach people about the history of rock and roll, and to inspire both musicians and fans.

Back in the Caribbean, the band finished up their *Steel Wheels* album. They were ready to tour again.

The Stones wanted the *Steel Wheels* tour to be bigger and better than anything they had done before. They had two stages built.

As they performed on one, the other stage could be on its way to the next stadium. It took a crew and staff of hundreds and more than fifty tractor-trailer trucks to move the tour around. The huge set looked like an old steel mill towering over the stage. It had giant video screens, strobe lights, smoke, and a wall of fire. The show ended with fireworks.

Nineteen eighty-nine was quite a year. The Stones had a successful comeback tour. They performed sixty shows in three and a half months. The tour earned $140 million. They were now members of the Rock and Roll Hall of Fame.

Rolling Stone magazine readers voted them the best artists, the best band, and the best tour of the year. Their time apart in the 1980s had been good for the Rolling Stones. Keith said, "We needed a break to find out what you can and what you can't do on your own. . . . Maybe that's the way to keep the band together: leaving for a bit."

But the Stones weren't simply keeping the band together. They had become the greatest rock-and-roll band in the world. And they were ready to keep rolling.

CHAPTER 9
Fifty Years and Counting

By the early 1990s, the Stones had been playing together for thirty years. This new decade brought some changes to the band. Bill Wyman decided to leave the Stones. Charlie released a solo jazz album with the Charlie Watts Orchestra. Ron, Mick, and Keith each released solo albums. Ron, who had always been an artist, held exhibitions of his paintings.

But the band was unstoppable. They signed a multimillion dollar record deal with Virgin Records. In 1994, they toured for their album *Voodoo Lounge*, with Darryl Jones replacing Bill.

During that tour, one of their Dallas performances became the first major live concert to be streamed over the Internet. The album won them a Grammy, an award given for outstanding work in the music industry, for best rock album.

Once that world tour ended, they started another tour to promote their album *Bridges to Babylon*.

The band was still going strong. The Stones were all in their fifties. They seemed to have more energy than ever before. When someone asked if this tour was their last one, Keith answered, "Yes—and the next five." The Stones continued to work hard to write music, make albums, and perform for fans.

They released albums and held large-scale tours into the 2000s. In 2002, the Rolling Stones released *Forty Licks* to mark their forty years together. No other rock band in the world had played together that long. Their *Bigger Bang* tour lasted for two years, from August 2005 to August 2007. It included the halftime show at the 2006 Super Bowl in Detroit, Michigan. On the football field, they played on a stage shaped like their own logo: a gigantic lips and tongue.

The tour included 147 concerts to about four and a half million people in thirty-two countries around the world. The band kept on doing what they did best: playing rock and roll.

Dread Pirate Richards

Keith Richards's well-known style—head scarf, earrings, black eye makeup, and silver rings—became the inspiration for Johnny Depp's character, Captain Jack Sparrow, in the Pirates of the Caribbean movies. In 2008, Keith himself appeared as Captain Jack's father in the third movie, *Pirates of the Caribbean: At World's End.*

In 2012, the Rolling Stones had been playing together for half a century. Most of the band members were almost in their seventies. They were millionaires. But their touring days were not over. To celebrate the band's fiftieth anniversary, they set out on their "50 & Counting" tour.

The tour started with a performance at the Marquee Club, where they had first played together as teenagers back in 1962.

The Rolling Stones have often been asked how long they thought the band would continue playing together. In a 1971 interview, Mick said that he had thought they might last for two years. Looking ahead, he added, "I'd rather be dead than sing 'Satisfaction' when I'm forty-five."

But the Rolling Stones are still playing "Satisfaction." Their love of music led them to become one of the most powerful forces in entertainment, and the greatest rock-and-roll band in the world.

Timeline of the Rolling Stones' Career

1936	Bass player Bill Wyman born on October 24 in London, England
1941	Drummer Charlie Watts born on June 2 in London, England
1942	Guitarist Brian Jones born on February 28 in Cheltenham, England
1943	Singer Mick Jagger born on July 26 in Dartford, England
	Guitarist Keith Richards born on December 18 in Dartford, England
1947	Bassist Ron Wood born June 1 in London, England
1961	Childhood friends Mick and Keith meet at the Dartford train station and realize they like the same types of music
1962	The Rollin' Stones play together for the first time at London's Marquee Club on July 12
1963	The band plays at the Crawdaddy Club on February 24
	In April, they sign on with manager Andrew Oldham, who gets them their first record deal
	On June 7, their first single is released
1964	Their first album, *The Rolling Stones*, is released on April 16
	They set off on their first US tour in June
1965	"(I Can't Get No) Satisfaction" released on June 6 and becomes a worldwide number-one hit

1969 — Brian Jones dies July 3

— Mick Taylor joins the Rolling Stones

— Concert at Altamont Speedway in California ends in violence on December 6

1971 — The Rolling Stones leave England for tax reasons and move to France

— Mick Taylor leaves the band

1972 — The Rolling Stones tongue-and-lips logo debuts on the album *Sticky Fingers*

1975 — Ron Wood joins the Rolling Stones

1989 — The Rolling Stones are inducted into the Rock and Roll Hall of Fame

2002 — The Rolling Stones release *Forty Licks* to celebrate forty years together

2012 — The Rolling Stones celebrate fifty years together as a band

— Their "50 & Counting" tour begins at the Marquee Club where the band first performed in 1962

2013 — The Rolling Stones are the main performers at Glastonbury Festival on June 29 in Somerset, England

Timeline of the World

1939	The movie *Gone with the Wind* premieres in the United States
1940	The German bombing of London during World War II—called the Blitz—lasts for fifty-seven days
1956	Construction of the interstate highway system begins in the United States
1957	Soviet space satellite *Sputnik 1*, launched on October 4, is the first object sent into orbit around Earth
1962	Artist Andy Warhol exhibits his famous soup can paintings in Los Angeles, California
1968	Civil rights leader Martin Luther King Jr. is killed on April 4 in Memphis, Tennessee
1969	The Woodstock festival, an outdoor concert in upstate New York, becomes a symbol of the peace-loving mood of the 1960s
1970	Earth Day is celebrated for the first time on April 22
1993	Web browsers give people access to the Internet, connecting them with information and to one another through their computers
2001	On September 11, terrorists attack the World Trade Center towers in New York City and the Pentagon outside Washington, DC
2015	The horse American Pharoah wins the three races to earn the Triple Crown, which had not been awarded in thirty-seven years

Bibliography

Davis, Stephen. ***Old Gods Almost Dead: The 40-Year Odyssey of the Rolling Stones***. New York: Broadway Books, 2001.

Forntale, Pete. ***50 Licks: Myths and Stories from Half a Century of The Rolling Stones***. New York: Bloomsbury, 2013.

George-Warren, Holly, Patricia R. Bashe, and Jon Pareles, eds. ***The Rolling Stone Encyclopedia of Rock & Roll***. New York: Fireside, 2001.

Jagger, Mick, Keith Richards, Charlie Watts, and Ron Wood. ***The Rolling Stones 50***. New York: Hyperion, 2012.

Loewenstein, Dora, and Philip Dodd, eds. ***According to the Rolling Stones***. San Francisco: Chronicle Books, 2003.

McMillian, John Campbell. ***Beatles vs. Stones***. New York: Simon & Schuster, 2013.

Morgen, Brett, director. ***Crossfire Hurricane***. London: Eagle Rock Entertainment, 2012.

Palmer, Robert. ***The Rolling Stones***. New York: Rolling Stone Press, 1983.

Richards, Keith. ***Life***. New York: Little, Brown & Company, 2010.

Rock and Roll Hall of Fame. "The Rolling Stones Biography." Accessed July 2015. http://rockhall.com/inductees/the-rolling-stones/bio.

"The Rolling Stones." ***Rolling Stone Magazine***. Accessed July 2015. http://www.rollingstone.com/music/artists/the-rolling-stones.

Scorsese, Martin, director. ***Shine a Light***. Hollywood, CA: Paramount Home Entertainment, 2008.